IMAGES
of America

WICHITA'S
LEGACY OF FLIGHT

IMAGES
of America

WICHITA'S
LEGACY OF FLIGHT

The American Institute of Aeronautics and
Astronautics–Wichita Section

Project Team:

John D. Hays   Benjamin Hruska
Chad Kannady   Charles J. Lawrence
Ben Matthaei   Jay M. Price
Sandra Reddish   Theresa St. Romain

ⒹAIAA

American Institute of Aeronautics and Astronautics

**CELEBRATING THE EVOLUTION OF FLIGHT
1903 TO 2003 ... AND BEYOND**

A

ARCADIA
PUBLISHING

Published by Arcadia Publishing
Charleston, South Carolina

Library of Congress Catalog Card Number: 2003109049

For all general information contact Arcadia Publishing at:
Telephone 843-853-2070
Fax 843-853-0044
E-mail sales@arcadiapublishing.com
For customer service and orders:
Toll-Free 1-888-313-2665

Visit us on the Internet at www.arcadiapublishing.com

CONTENTS

ACKNOWLEDGMENTS

This book recognizes Wichita's contributions to aviation history and documents the ways in which aviation transformed Wichita. It would not have been possible without the support of the American Institute of Aeronautics and Astronautics (AIAA). Both the national and regional units of AIAA provided the support for this project, which is part of the AIAA's commemoration of the centennial of flight. The project team that did the work of putting this book together were students with the Public History Program at Wichita State University. The students were John D. Hays, Benjamin Hruska, Chad Kannady, Charles J. Lawrence, Ben Matthaei, Sandra Reddish, and Theresa St. Romain. They brought to the project a wide range of skills and backgrounds, yet all shared an enthusiasm for tackling this complex community history. Aaron Morris and Margaret Kline were the official liaisons for AIAA. Jay M. Price administered the project.

The project team is very appreciative for all the assistance and patience from the staff of the Kansas Aviation Museum; Wichita State University Libraries, Department of Special Collections; the Wichita-Sedgwick County Historical Museum; and the Wichita Public Library, Local History Section. Thanks also to Wichita Eagle and Beacon Publishing Company, the Wichita Chamber of Commerce, Bombardier, Cessna, Raytheon, Boeing, the Butler County Historical Society, and other companies and organizations that helped with research and allowed the use of images and text for the book. The project team also thanks the many friends, family, and colleagues who have all been supportive and valuable sounding boards for this endeavor. Finally, thanks goes to all of the photographers, both amateur and professional, who produced the images that appear in this book.

INTRODUCTION

Two brothers from Dayton, Ohio, changed the world when they first flew on December 17, 1903, at Kitty Hawk, North Carolina. What no one realized at the time was that they had also forever changed the face of a burgeoning city on the Great Plains—Wichita, Kansas. Wichita, the "Magic City," the "Peerless Princess of the Plains," the "Great Empire of the Southwest" was about to become "The Air Capital of the World."

Wichita had changed its image several times before 1903. It began as a cattle town and trading center. It then became a center for agriculture and entrepreneurism, capitalizing on its location within the "bread basket" of the United States, and encouraging business start-ups such as Coleman and Mentholatum. This entrepreneurial spirit spilled over into Wichita's leisure time. Balloon races were the rage in the 1910s, but lost their novelty when airplanes began flying into town. Wichitans fell in love with the new, romantic, and often dangerous mode of transportation. They could not get enough of fliers like Kingman County resident Clyde Cessna, who thrilled audiences in his airplane and later founded one of the hallmarks of American aviation, Cessna Aircraft Company. Walter Beech, along with Clyde Cessna, was a co-founder of Travel Air. Beech received his first paying aircraft job in Wichita by dropping pro-Southwestern College leaflets over Fairmount College before a Fairmount vs. Southwestern football game in 1920. He went on to found Beech Aircraft Company.

World War I proved that the newfangled machines were good for something other than crowd-pleasing. Wichita had become prosperous thanks to the discovery of oil in the area, and the oilmen saw aviation as one of many viable investments. Soon, the city was dotted with aircraft companies such as Stearman, Travel Air, Cessna, and Swallow, funded through these investors. These companies grew into the aviation giants of Beech, Boeing and Cessna. Later on, another company, Learjet, joined Wichita's aviation community.

Wichita made its mark on aviation, but the reverse was also true. Aviation became Wichita's largest employer by the end of World War II. The aircraft workers lived in housing developments named Beechwood and Planeview. They deposited their money into Air Capital Savings and received loans from Air Capital Pawn Shop when economic times dictated. Students, alumni, and civic groups held their reunions and celebrations in the Cessna Activity Center or Walter Beech Hall. They watched football games at Wichita State University's Cessna Stadium.

The aircraft industry was not just about building planes, however. Supporting companies such as avionics manufacturers, parts manufacturers, and custom interior shops resided in Wichita because of its aviation heritage. Local air carriers such as Central Air Lines and Ryan International sprang up in the fertile field of Wichita aviation. McConnell Air Force Base alone infused millions of dollars into the economy when it was built in the 1950s, and gave welcome work to area contractors. Wichita Mid-Continent Airport saw its passenger numbers more than double in the 1970s, although changing patterns in air travel caused many travelers to fly from other airports during the 1990s.

Wichita had some tumultuous times during the first century of flight. The roller-coaster aircraft industry—slave to the whims of military and commercial airline contracts as well as fickle business aircraft customers—caused a similar roller-coaster in Wichita's economy. When the industry boomed, so did the city. When the industry lagged, Wichita's unemployment jumped, causing scores of workers and their families to leave Wichita for better opportunities.

Despite the boom and bust nature of aviation, Wichita has maintained its affiliation. Oil and agriculture are still an important part of Wichita's economy, as evidenced by Koch Industries and Garvey Grain. New businesses such as Pizza Hut, Rent-A-Center, and White Castle gave periodic employment to Wichitans. The city became a major regional medical center in the 1980s to offset some of its dependence on aviation.

Yet aviation was still the dominant industry in the "Air Capital." The purpose of this book is to commemorate the first century of flight. There could be no better way to tell the story of aviation's impact on Wichita and its people than through their photographs.

One

TAKING FLIGHT

By the turn of the twentieth century, the city of Wichita had already seen several significant boom and bust cycles in the town's 30-year existence. The short but wild cattle drive era began with the arrival of the railroad in 1872, and ended with the movement of the Texas longhorn quarantine line further west a few years later. Land speculation caused a real estate boom in the 1880s that collapsed in 1887 and was closely followed by a national depression in the 1890s. Wichita was a business-minded place and when the town began to recover at the turn of the century the community leaders were hungry for new business ventures. The dawn of the aviation age started at Kitty Hawk on December 17, 1903 and provided Wichita with a new vision. Within 25 years of that first flight, Wichita had become the producer of one-fourth of all commercially-built planes in the United States, with over 25 aircraft companies. There were a number of reasons for this prominence: a central location, flat terrain, and a sunny, breezy climate conducive to flying nearly year-round. However, it was the confluence of abundant investment capital made in nearby oil fields, hard-working mechanical inventiveness nurtured on prosperous Kansas farms, and the knack for self-promotion and boosterism that made Wichita the Air Capital of the World.

Pictured is the National Balloon Race of 1915. (Courtesy Wichita Public Library, Local History Section.)

This "bird's-eye" view is an artist's conception of turn-of-the-century Wichita, just before the population climbed to 34,000 in 1905, finally regaining the thousands lost during the recent bust years. Business prospects rose and Wichita expanded its interests as a center for agricultural supply, milling, and the broom corn industry. It became involved in new ventures such as A.A. Hyde's Mentholatum and the Coleman Company. "Watch Wichita Win" was the slogan for renewed Wichita self-promotion. The city built the Forum downtown for the hosting of trade shows and sent a railroad car full of boosters to surrounding states with the Wichita Trade Excursion. Promotion of the airplane industry began with demonstrations and air shows. This booster spirit eventually brought most of the early aviation leaders to town and turned Wichita into the Air Capital. (Courtesy Wichita State University Libraries, Department of Special Collections.)

From May 4 to May 6, 1911, the Walnut Grove Air Meet entertained between 12,000 and 18,000 spectators. This Curtiss Biplane, flown by Eugene Ely, was the first aircraft photographed in Wichita. Ely attempted to set a new altitude record before running out of fuel at 7,000 feet. The thousands of Wichitans present traveled to the field north of town by automobile or in special railcars. (Courtesy Wichita State University Libraries, Department of Special Collections.)

Although the thought of flight intrigued some, the surrounding community remained firmly grounded in agriculture as behemoth tractors and threshing machines made a presence on family farms. (Courtesy Wichita Public Library, Local History Section.)

Ackerman's Island in Wichita was home to the Wonderland amusement park and a baseball stadium. During the 1908 "Peerless Prophets' Jubilee" fair, Wichitans received their first taste of flight when fair organizers brought the Knabenshue Airship to town in an attempt to link the city with aviation. After several abortive attempts to fly around city hall, the 150-foot dirigible crash-landed and was destroyed, a victim of the Kansas wind. (Courtesy Wichita State University Libraries, Department of Special Collections.)

The Wichita Aero Club raised the money to bring the National Balloon Races to Wichita in 1915. About 14,000 people attended this three-day event on Ackerman's Island to witness the assent of the balloons that competed for greatest distance traveled. Other contests included a race between a car, driven by Barney Oldfield, and a biplane, flown by De Lloyd Thompson. (Courtesy Wichita Public Library, Local History Section.)

12

William Coffin Coleman started his own company in 1901, leasing and servicing gasoline lamps in communities with unreliable or nonexistent electric utilities. In 1903, he began to produce his own lantern, eventually marketing that and many other products around the world. This picture shows a group of Coleman employees enjoying a game of volleyball at a company sponsored picnic at Wichita's Linwood Park. (Courtesy Wichita-Sedgwick County Historical Museum.)

The Crawford Grand Opera House developed from the great Wichita land speculation boom of the 1880s. Completed in 1887 and located on the corner of Topeka and William Streets, it held over 1500 patrons. The facility was renamed the Lyceum in 1911 and, as shown in this picture, was destroyed in a fire on April 1, 1913. (Courtesy Wichita Public Library, Local History Section.)

Clyde Cessna grew up on a farm southwest of Wichita in Kingman County. A gifted mechanic, his first plane was *Silverwing*, a Bleriot-style monoplane produced by Queen Aeroplane Company in New York. Cessna learned to rebuild and improve the aircraft's design through successive crashes and made demonstration flights at fairs and flying exhibitions throughout Kansas and Oklahoma. Encouraged by local promoters, Cessna produced the *Comet*, the first aircraft built in Wichita in 1917. Cessna shared factory space with Wichita's Jones 6 automobile plant. The buildings originally housed the Burton Car Works, which produced livestock transport rail cars around 1890. This picture of Cessna seated in the *Comet* shows the early development of an enclosed cockpit and Cessna's preference for monoplanes in the age of biplanes. Some early versions of the *Comet* carried advertising for local companies painted on the underside of the wing. Efforts to build airplanes stalled briefly during World War I after Cessna was unable to gain government contracts. (Courtesy Kansas Aviation Museum.)

The first flights of Clyde Cessna's *Silverwing* took place from the salt flats of northern Oklahoma in 1911. Three days later, the original *Silverwing* was nearly destroyed in a crash, causing injury to the pilot and the cancellation of booked demonstration flights. Repairing and rebuilding the craft after crashes provided the expertise Cessna needed to become an aircraft designer and manufacturer. (Courtesy Kansas Aviation Museum.)

In April 1917, the U.S. entered into the great European war. Initially, thousands of men volunteered for service to go "over there" to fight the Germans. One was Edwin Bleckley, a second lieutenant in the Kansas National Guard and Wichita native, who soon found himself attached to the 130th Field Artillery unit in France. Once in France, he volunteered for the Air Service as an aerial observer and by August 1918, attached to the 50th Aero Squadron, was ready for combat duty. On October 6, 1918, Bleckley and his pilot, Lieutenant Goettler, found themselves flying over heavily wooded terrain to search and drop supplies for Major Whittlesey's "Lost Battalion," which was surrounded by German soldiers. This trip met with disaster when their plane was shot down, killing both men. Goettler and Bleckley received the Congressional Medal of Honor posthumously. (Courtesy Wichita-Sedgwick County Historical Museum.)

Women and men of Wichita did their part in supporting the war effort. For women, the most popular uniforms would be those of Red Cross workers, while the men exchanged their civilian clothes for khakis. (Courtesy Wichita-Sedgwick County Museum and Wichita Public Library, Local History Section.)

Jake Moellendick is often called the father of Wichita aviation. After making his fortune in the El Dorado oil fields, Moellendick brought to town important men in Wichita aviation history, such as Matty Laird. Almost as legendary as his business acumen was his abrasive personality, which eventually caused his core talent to split off and form two of the three major aircraft companies in Wichita. (Courtesy Wichita Public Library, Local History Section.)

Black Gold! With the discovery of enormous oil fields, Wichita and surrounding communities profited from this new found and seemingly endless wealth. Money made from the oil fields soon made its way into financing another budding industry: aircraft manufacturing. (Courtesy Butler County Historical Society.)

Oilman Jake Moellendick (standing) and Oklahoma car dealer Buck Weaver persuaded Emil M. "Matty" Laird (in the cockpit) to move his company to Wichita from Chicago. Laird stayed in Wichita for only three years but left behind an aircraft legacy. The Laird Swallow was the first aircraft manufactured in Wichita in large numbers. The E.M. Laird Company, maker of the Swallow, brought others to Wichita, including Walter Beech and Lloyd Stearman, who, along with Clyde Cessna, led Wichita into its aviation future. The Laird Swallow was the first production-built aircraft for commercial use. In 1920, about 15 Laird Swallows had been produced and sold. (Courtesy Wichita Public Library, Local History Section.)

With the "war to end all wars" finished, Kansas, like the rest of the country, soon turned its energies to frivolity. Wichita staged 'Bathing Beauty' contests and sent one of its own beauties, a young Louise Brooks, on to fame and fortune in Hollywood and the silent movies. (Courtesy Wichita-Sedgwick County Historical Museum and Wichita Public Library, Local History Section.)

In 1926, Fairmount College, founded in 1895, became the University of Wichita and the first city college west of the Mississippi River. The early years of the new university brought increased enrollment, larger faculty, and added programs. In 1928, the university opened its Aeronautical Engineering Department, one of only six in the nation and the only engineering discipline offered on campus at the time. Fairmount Hall, shown here, burned down in 1929. (Courtesy Wichita State University Libraries, Department of Special Collections.)

"Princess Wichita," locally known as Miss Gladys Martin, presided over the National Air Congress held on an October weekend in 1924 at the new municipal airfield in the "California" section, six miles southeast of downtown. The local chapter of the National Aeronautical Association raised $20,000 to bring the congress to town and offered $10,000 in prize money for a variety of flying competitions. The event was delayed for a day due to torrential rains but drew 8,000 spectators on Saturday and 25,000 on Sunday. Local newspaper headlines read "Wichita the Capital City of Aviation World Today" and covered the event extensively with numerous articles and photographs. The event included air races and barnstormer stunt flying, attracting participants from all over the United States with the intent of promoting Wichita as a national center of aviation. The *Eagle* later reported "Wichita has climbed on the aviation map. The public will see that it doesn't get off." (Courtesy Kansas Aviation Museum.)

With a growing workforce, new neighborhoods developed throughout Wichita. Executives and managers lived in fashionable homes in College Hill. Workers lived in more modest homes in College Hill (as pictured above), as well as in Riverside, along the Arkansas River; Delano, to the west of downtown; and in neighborhoods on the city's southern edge. Many lived in "airplane bungalows," named for the rear "wing" consisting of a raised room designed to catch summer breezes. (Courtesy Jay M. Price.)

Edgar B. Smith was a Wichita commercial photographer from the 1920s to the 1950s. He learned to fly in 1917 at Clyde Cessna's flying school and used his WWI vintage Standard J-1 biplane to take aerial photography. Smith was responsible for the photographic documentation of much of Wichita's history. (Courtesy Wichita-Sedgwick County Historical Museum.)

After the departure of Matty Laird from Wichita, Laird Aircraft was reformed as the Swallow Airplane Manufacturing Company, headed by Jake Moellendick. Lloyd Stearman was chief engineer and Walter Beech was manager of flight operations. This view shows a Swallow flying over the factory on North Hillside. Stearman and Beech soon left the company to start Travel Air with Clyde Cessna. (Courtesy Kansas Aviation Museum.)

This 1928 photograph shows skilled Swallow Aircraft workers building lightweight wing rib trusses out of wood fastened together with tacks. By 1929, Wichita aircraft manufacturers employed 2,000 workers producing 1,000 airplanes, about 26 percent of all U.S. aircraft production. The city also boasted its own airline and 13 flying schools. (Courtesy Kansas Aviation Museum.)

Victor Roos, shown seated in a Swallow aircraft, first became involved in Wichita aircraft business when he formed the Cessna-Roos Aircraft Company with Clyde Cessna in 1927. He became the manager of a newly reorganized Swallow Aircraft Company later that same year. (Courtesy Kansas Aviation Museum.)

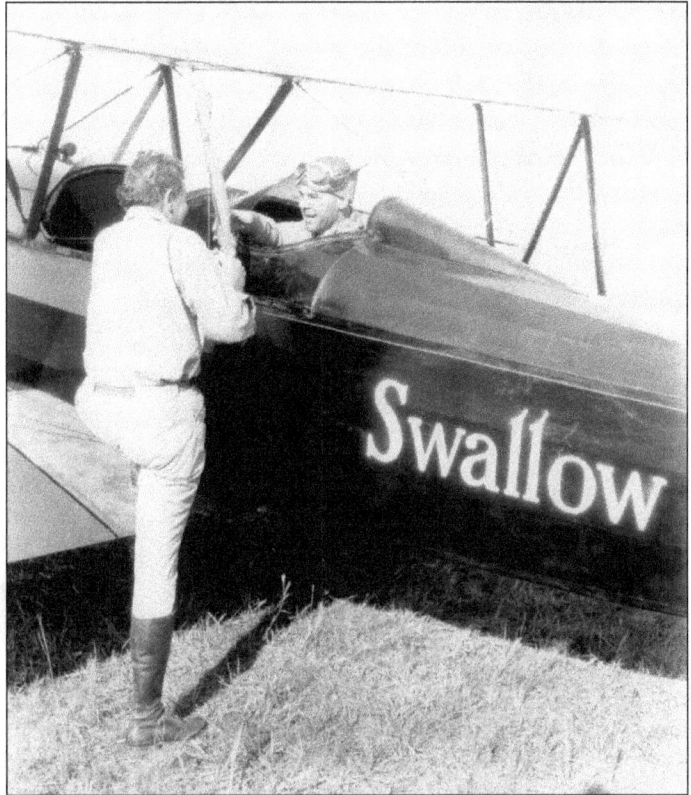

What better way to promote *Wings*, the sensational hit movie of 1927, than by having a Wichita produced Swallow plane on display in Chicago? Of course, having gangster-like dandies with spats sitting in front of the plane could only enhance 1920s Chicago's "tough guy" image. (Courtesy Kansas Aviation Museum.)

In 1924, Lloyd Stearman and Walter Beech left Swallow and in 1925, joined with Clyde Cessna to form Travel Air. Stearman left the company in 1926. Cessna left in 1927, before Beech moved the company to a new facility on East Central. These aircraft designers are shown in the drafting room of the new facility. (Courtesy Kansas Aviation Museum.)

A Travel Air Model A flies over the new factory on East Central, the site of the future Beech Aircraft Company. Adjacent to the facility was the Wichita Booster Club airfield that hosted events such as the Ford Reliability Tour, a national air rally designed to boost public confidence in flying. (Courtesy Kansas Aviation Museum.)

Airplanes were taking off to the stars as actor Wallace Beery and cowboy star Ken Maynard stop by Wichita to shop for that special plane to take back to Hollywood. Beery's chosen plane was a top-of-the-line Travel Air that cost $20,000 in 1928. (Courtesy Kansas Aviation Museum.)

The Braley Flying School owned this Travel Air 2000, photographed in 1928. The school included its own airport for pilot training, a factory for instruction in aircraft manufacture, and a dormitory for students to live in. The school produced several of their own aircraft such as the *Breezle Bug* biplane. The facility was located on East Franklin Road (now Pawnee). (Courtesy Kansas Aviation Museum.)

Controversial doctor, radio station operator, and almost Kansas governor John R. Brinkley (on the right) is shown in front of a Travel Air 6000 aircraft holding copies of the *Wichita Beacon* headlining his visit to Wichita. Brinkley gained fame by claiming to restore virility to men by implanting goat glands. In 1930, he launched a write-in campaign for governor but lost due to "irregularities" in counting the votes. (Courtesy Kansas Aviation Museum.)

Why drive when you can fly? Air travel became an alternative mode of transporting sporting teams from city to city and left the long bus rides along the dusty roads. The Travel Air baseball team not only took advantage of air travel, but promoted its company name and products by playing the game. (Courtesy Kansas Aviation Museum.)

There were many factors that led to Wichita becoming the Air Capital besides the incredible talent and genius of its citizens, and one of those factors was the location. Wide open spaces and nothing to run into for miles around made Wichita ideal for pilots. (Courtesy Kansas Aviation Museum.)

After forming Cessna Aircraft Company in 1927 (first named Cessna-Roos) Clyde Cessna developed several successful monoplanes such as the Model AW and Model BW. Cessna also developed a line of racing planes. A proposal from the Curtiss Flying Service in 1929 calling for the production of 50 planes per month prompted Cessna to relocate to a new facility on Franklin Road (Pawnee) just prior to the stock market crash of October 1929. The facility closed in January 1931. (Both Courtesy Kansas Aviation Museum.)

Clyde Cessna's son Eldon is shown piloting a glider designed to be launched by bungee cord or by being towed by an automobile. The gliders sold for $398 in 1930 and were an attempt to revitalize the sagging Depression-era aircraft business. About 300 of the units were sold in a prefabricated form. (Courtesy Kansas Aviation Museum.)

After closing the East Franklin plant, Clyde and Eldon Cessna opened a smaller facility on South Oliver to design and build racing planes. This CR-3 is shown with pilot and co-designer Johnny Livingston, who used the plane to set several speed records in Depression-Era air races. (Courtesy Kansas Aviation Museum.)

Walter Anderson, a short order cook, and real estate and insurance salesman Billy Ingram became partners in several Wichita hamburger stands, which in 1924 became the "White Castle System of Eating Houses." An example of one is in the lower right corner of this picture. The company trademark was a symbol of cleanliness and purity. In the 1930s, Anderson sold his share of White Castle to Ingram, who moved the headquarters to Ohio. (Courtesy Wichita-Sedgwick County Historical Museum.)

Walter Anderson (on right), co-founder of the White Castle chain of restaurants, also started Swift Aircraft. The company was founded in 1927 and built less than a dozen Swift Sports before the Great Depression put the company out of business. (Courtesy Kansas Aviation Museum.)

Twenty-five planes participated in the All-Kansas Air Tour in 1928, which flew a circuit around Kansas to promote aviation and airport construction. Kansas Governor Ben Palen participated in the tour. Appropriately, Quick Air Motors, also of Wichita, made the engine for some of the airplanes. (Courtesy Kansas Aviation Museum.)

By the mid-1920s, welded metal framework began to replace wood in aircraft structure. Metal was more reliable and required less skill and handwork than wood. After a short period of training in the art of welding, perhaps at a local flying school, a worker was qualified to produce standardized parts to blueprint specifications. (Courtesy Kansas Aviation Museum.)

Watkins Aircraft, located on the corner of Douglas and Spruce, produced a two-seat, all-plywood monoplane called the Skylark. Everett A. Watkins also ran the Universal Flying School, the Watkins Manufacturing Company, and the Central Airlines Company. The building in the picture still stands across from Wichita High School East and houses a photographic business. (Courtesy Kansas Aviation Museum.)

The booming Wichita aircraft industry of the 1920s spawned other supporting businesses. M.J. "Pop" Stone's propeller factory was largely a family business run by Stone and his four sons. The business, located at Lincoln and Washington, became the Supreme Propeller Company. (Courtesy Kansas Aviation Museum.)

Eager to show the advantages of air travel to the residents of Kansas's outlying areas, this Travel Air biplane demonstrated that it was capable of landing in a field to deliver parts for a waiting wheat harvesting crew. (Courtesy Wichita State University Libraries, Department of Special Collections.)

As the aviation craze swept the country, Wichita celebrated its new-found industry by welcoming two of the biggest names in the country: Amelia Earhart and Charles Lindbergh. Here Amelia Earhart receives a happy welcome from oil man and aviation financial supporter Jake Moellendick. (Courtesy Wichita State University Libraries, Department of Special Collections.)

Charles Lindbergh and Walter Beech shared not only an interest in flying, but comfort with the camera. (Courtesy Wichita Public Library, Local History Section.)

The first Nu-Way Sandwich Shop opened on West Douglas Avenue in 1928, serving up its specialty loose-meat hamburgers. Fast-food lunch counters became popular in an era when men and women began to commute on streetcars from surrounding areas to the downtown, too far to return home for lunch. Nu-Way was one of several fast food franchise restaurants that began in Wichita, including White Castle and Pizza Hut. (Courtesy Wichita State University Libraries, Department of Special Collections and Wichita Public Library, Local History Section.)

With local boosterism becoming contagious, the public embraced the slogan "The Air Capital," and the related logo of a sunflower sprouting wings. People could show off their civic pride by attaching specially-made emblems onto the grills of their automobiles. (Courtesy Wichita-Sedgwick County Museum and John D. Hays.)

In 1931, Wichita hosted the Southwestern Lumbermen's Association conference. Specially-made name tag holders for the participants showed off Kansas products such as oil, wheat, and airplanes. (Courtesy John D. Hays.)

Roughly 2,000 participants and wives gathered in Wichita for the Southwestern Lumbermen's Association conference, causing a scramble for hotel rooms. Benefits for wives accompanying their husbands included free airplane rides over Wichita. (Courtesy Kansas Aviation Museum.)

Even as the Great Depression started to grip the country, people found ways to escape from the daily grind. Movies became a popular form of relief. For those who preferred outdoor entertainment, there were sports such as baseball. Wichitans were no different, except the daily sight of watching planes in the air gave them an extra bit of enjoyment. The occasional airplane crash was another form of diversion as people mingled around the wreckage in amazement. If the pilot could walk away, and even pose by the wreck, that was just an extra treat for spectators. (Courtesy Kansas Aviation Museum.)

Two

"To the Stars Through Difficulties"

The stock market crash of October 1929 and the onset of the Great Depression ended the aviation boom in Wichita and put many companies out of business. Just prior to the crash, two companies merged with larger conglomerates. Curtiss-Wright bought out Travel Air, and Walter Beech moved to its St. Louis headquarters. Short on orders, the former Travel Air factory shut down. United Aircraft and Transport Company bought Stearman. Cessna Aircraft closed its doors. However, these companies were soon reformed into businesses that hung on to become three of the major aircraft companies in the world.

Clyde Cessna regained control of his company and hired his nephew, University of Wichita aeronautical engineer Dwane Wallace. Wallace led the company for decades, building it into a leader in general aviation. Bouyed by the influx of capital from United Transport, Stearman moved to a new factory on South Oliver. When United Transport was broken up by an anti-trust measure, Stearman became part of the Seattle-based Boeing Company and eventually the Boeing Wichita Division. Walter Beech moved back from St. Louis and restarted Travel Air as Beech Aircraft Company in 1932. Rather than destroying these companies, hard times refined them into better and stronger businesses ready to accept the challenge and enormous growth that World War II brought. As a city, Wichita survived the Depression years and then withstood a boom that doubled its population in a few short years.

The Beech Model 18 is pictured above. (Courtesy Kansas Aviation Museum.)

In the foreground of this 1931 aerial view is the new Stearman plant, built on the site of the former Swift Company. An infusion of capital resulting from Stearman's merger with United Aircraft and Transport made the endeavor possible. This building, located on South Oliver, is still part of Boeing, known as Wichita Plant I. Stalled in its development by the Great Depression, the Wichita Municipal Airport stands in the background, awaiting completion of the terminal building. (Courtesy Kansas Aviation Museum.)

Varney Air Lines was one of the nation's first private companies contracted to carry the U.S. mail. Varney initially used six Swallow aircraft and eventually added other craft, such as this Stearman biplane. The company became part of Boeing Air Transport, which, like Stearman, was part of United Aircraft and Transport. After the split-up of United Aircraft, Varney became part of United Airlines. (Courtesy Kansas Aviation Museum.)

After Stearman became a division of the Boeing Company, it received an order for army trainers that carried the company through the Great Depression. Production of the Kaydet, shown lined up across from the plant on the other side of Oliver, began in 1933 and continued until 1945, after 8,431 of the aircraft were produced. Frustrated over the lack of control, Lloyd Stearman left the company in the early 1930s and became president of the Lockheed Aircraft Company. (Courtesy Wichita Public Library, Local History Section.)

The University of Wichita's Department of Aeronautical Engineering had its own aircraft, such as the one above, and had a wind tunnel for testing aircraft designs. Engineers working in the local aircraft industry taught many of the classes in local factories and machine shops to achieve a combination of practical experience and applied science. One of the school's earliest graduates was Dwane Wallace, who went on to lead Cessna Aircraft. (Courtesy Kansas Aviation Museum.)

After regaining control of his aircraft company, Clyde Cessna hired his nephew, Wichita University aeronautical engineering graduate Dwane Wallace. Wallace, standing second from right in this 1934 photo of the engineering test group, headed up the company until his retirement in 1975. Under his guidance, Cessna dominated the light aircraft business and became one of Wichita's top employers. (Courtesy Wichita State University Libraries, Department of Special Collections.)

Who said engineers didn't have a sense of humor? In spite of stereotypes to the contrary, aircraft engineers could be funny, as attested by cartoons such as these, portraying Stearman engineers and workers. (Courtesy Kansas Aviation Museum.)

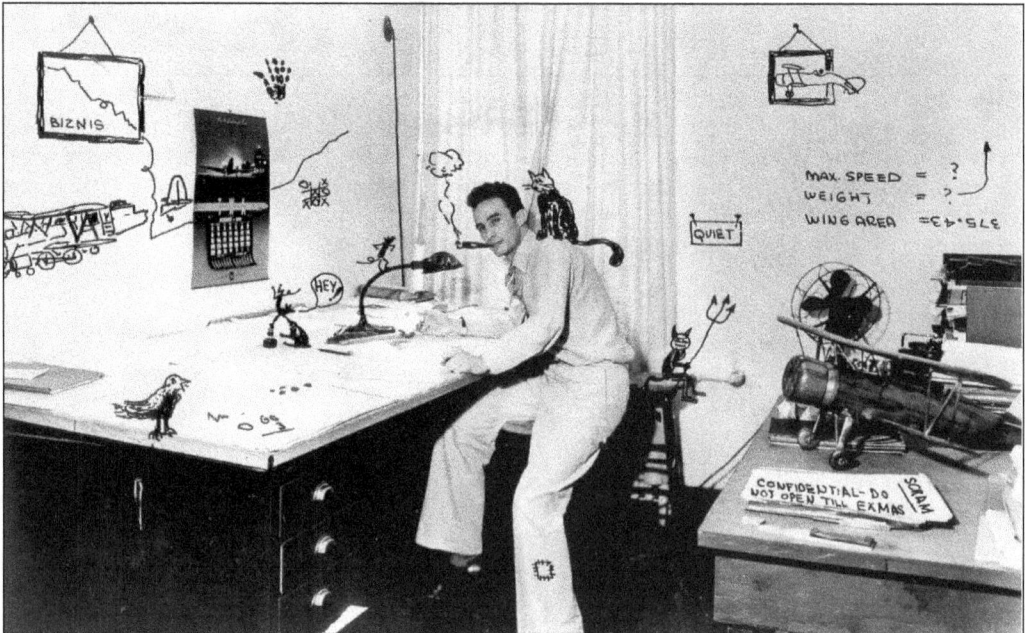

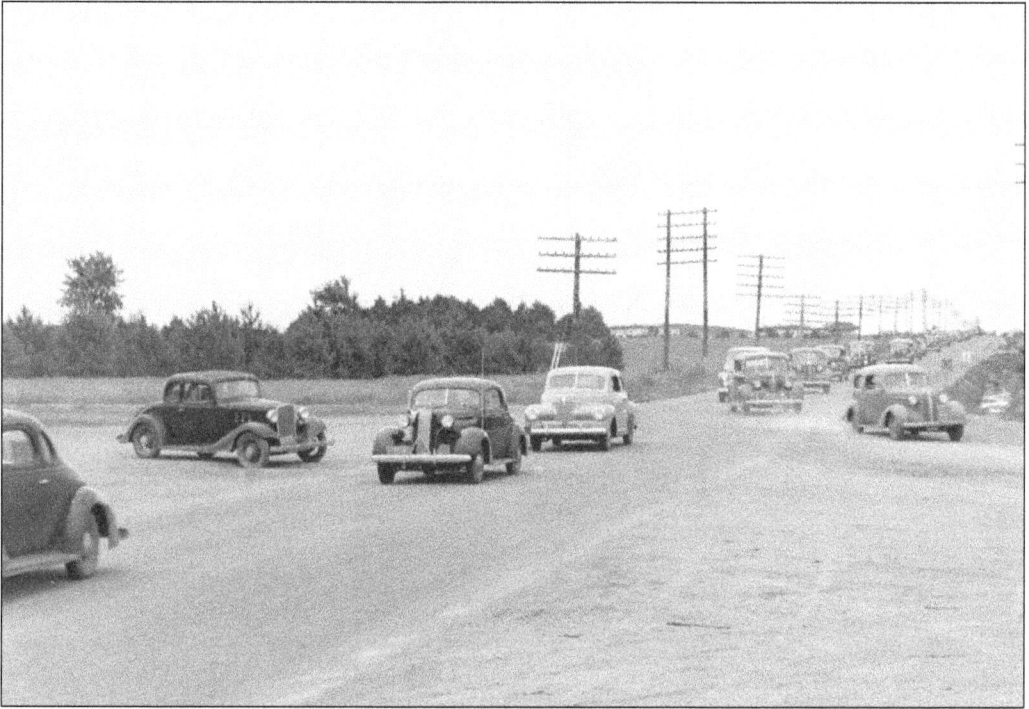

By the end of the 1930s, aircraft orders increased and people began going back to work. While glad to be working again, another irritation developed—traffic jams both to and from the job. (Courtesy Wichita Public Library, Local History Section.)

After a long day at the job, workers could head to the Grapevine for BBQ and beer. (Courtesy Wichita-Sedgwick County Historical Museum.)

Wiley Post was a pioneer aviator and the first to fly around the world in 1931, traveling over 15,000 miles in eight days in a Lockheed Vega nicknamed the *Winnie Mae*. Post also set altitude records in pressure suits of his own design and was the first to fly around the world solo. He was also a friend of American humorist Will Rogers, and they died together in a plane crash at Barrow, Alaska, on August 15, 1935. On June 15, two months prior to his fatal crash, Post made a dead-stick landing at Wichita after *Winnie Mae*'s engine failed during an attempt at a transcontinental stratospheric flight. Lloyd Stearman is on far right in the group photo. (Courtesy Wichita Public Library, Local History Section and Kansas Aviation Museum.)

Comedian and film star Bob Cummings was a life-long pilot. Here he proudly poses with his Cessna plane that he named the *Spinach II*. Cummings believed in and practiced a "health-food and vitamin" diet well before such practice was in vogue. (Courtesy Kansas Aviation Museum.)

Betty Browning of Kansas City won the 1936 Amelia Earhart Trophy at the Los Angeles National Air Races in her Cessna C-34. Like many other forms of entertainment, air races had their heyday during the Depression-era 1930s and Wichita airplanes built by Cessna and Beech dominated many competitions. (Courtesy Kansas Aviation Museum.)

Walter Beech, a founding member of Wichita's aviation industry, was born in Tennessee. He came to Wichita as a test pilot and salesman for the Laird Company before joining with Lloyd Stearman and Clyde Cessna to form Travel Air. Beech moved to St. Louis after Curtis-Wright purchased Travel Air, but returned to Wichita to form Beech Aircraft with his wife, Olive Ann. The company gained success with the Model 17 Staggerwing, a high-performance, race-winning aircraft. The Model 18 was a monoplane that developed into an important business workhorse, a World War II bomber trainer, and the first of a long line of successful Beech business planes. Walter Beech died in 1950, and Olive Ann continued to run the company until 1982. (Courtesy Wichita State University Libraries, Department of Special Collections.)

After developing the Model 17 Staggerwing in the Cessna Pawnee plant, Walter Beech moved his new company back to the former Travel Air facility on East Douglas. A Staggerwing poses in mid-flight over the newly painted Beech Aircraft sign in this 1934 photograph. Having started with only 10, the company had 250 employees by 1938. (Courtesy Kansas Aviation Museum.)

Although it never sold in large numbers during the Great Depression, the Beech Model 17 Staggerwing was a classic, high-performance racing plane. In 1936, a Staggerwing piloted by Wichitan Louise Thaden won the prestigious Bendix Trophy, flying from New York to Los Angeles in 14 hours and 55 minutes and averaging 165 miles per hour. The stylish aircraft also played an important role in several Hollywood movies, including *Too Hot to Handle* with Walter Pidgeon, Myrna Loy, and Clark Gable. (Courtesy Kansas Aviation Museum.)

In the 1920s, Wichita promoted itself as the airline crossroads of America, hoping to become the hub for airplanes flying cross-country or to Mexico. Wichita was a 10-hour flight from Los Angeles or 20 hours by plane and train from New York. Most of the early airlines passed through Wichita including Transcontinental Air Transport, Central Air Line, National Air Transportation, and Western Air Express. Large air transports could operate easily and safely out of the Wichita Municipal Airport because the grass field allowed take-off and landing in practically any direction. This Western Air Express Fokker F-32, stopped in Wichita for refueling, was the first four-engine airliner designed and built in the United States and could carry 30 passengers at 146 mph with a range of 740 miles. (Courtesy Wichita Public Library, Local History Section.)

The Wichita Municipal Airport was located six miles southeast of the center of town in the "California" section on 640 acres of prairie turf. This plot of ground was an important center of Wichita aviation, near the site of Swift Aircraft, Stearman, Cessna, and the Braley School of Flying, and eventually, the Boeing Company and McConnell Air Force Base as well. The facility operated out of this hangar beginning in 1929. The Depression stalled the opening of the Art Deco main terminal building until 1935. Wichita's airport was one of the busiest in the nation, but as planes became faster, larger, and safer, and increased their range, it became a fuel stop rather than a hub, losing out in importance to larger regional centers such as Kansas City. (Courtesy Kansas Aviation Museum.)

Wichitans liked to celebrate, and, as pictured in this photograph, they turned out at the Wichita Municipal Airport to welcome the new DC-3s from airline companies TWA, Braniff, and Central Air Lines. (Courtesy Kansas Aviation Museum.)

L.W. Clapp, former Wichita city manager and president of the park board, was a man of many talents. His watercolor sketch celebrating Charles Lindbergh's flight over the Atlantic became the colored frieze on the Municipal Airport building. Local lore says that the green in the mural came from crushed Mentholatum bottles. (Courtesy John D. Hays.)

Because of Wichita's location, it became a major stopover for flights such as the DC-3 above. For Wichitans, that meant a chance to see Hollywood celebrities, such as 1930s actress Eleanor Whitney. (Courtesy Kansas Aviation Museum.)

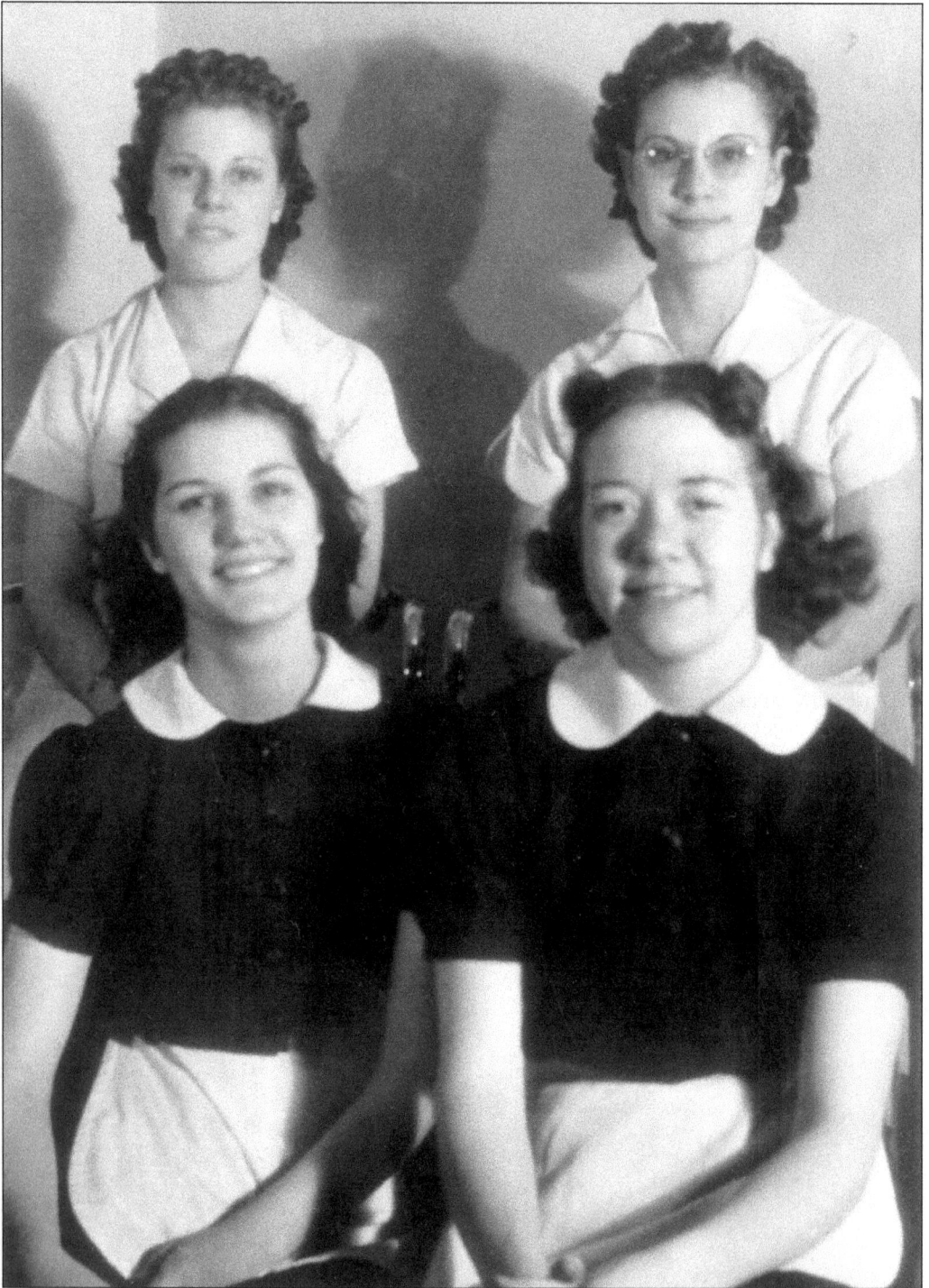

By the late 1930s, the Wichita airport offered its patrons some amenities as they waited for their planes or to see who would appear on the next flight. Customers had the option of either stopping by the soda fountain for quick refreshments or enjoying a full meal in the dining room. The friendly staff included these four women. (Courtesy Kansas Aviation Museum.)

U.S.S. WICHITA - LAUNCHING
VESSEL ENTERING DOCK FOR
REMOVAL OF CRADLE.
NAVY YARD, PHILA., NOV 16 1937
724-37-N.

In 1937, the heavy cruiser U.S.S. *Wichita* left the Philadelphia Naval yards ready to be outfitted for life on the high seas. When the United States entered World War II in 1941, the U.S.S. *Wichita* was ready for action. By the time the war ended in 1945, the U.S.S. *Wichita* had participated in both the Atlantic and Pacific theaters. The citizens of Wichita participated in the war in many ways. Men and women joined the Armed Forces to defeat the Axis Powers. People on the homefront also pulled together and did 'their part' for the war effort by saving scraps and buying war bonds. Companies, from Beech and Boeing and Cessna to Rawdon and Culver, were part of wartime aircraft production. Coleman produced goods for GIs while farmers grew the grain that fed the troops. (Courtesy Wichita-Sedgwick County Historical Museum.)

The U.S. Army Air Corps found Wichita an ideal location for producing their planes at rapid rates, and many Air Corps representatives became very familiar with the city. (Courtesy Kansas Aviation Museum.)

A blight on American society at this time was the practice of segregation of the races. However, one location where this was not adhered to was at the canteen located in the Union Station. (Courtesy Wichita-Sedgwick County Historical Museum.)

Communities throughout America worked together in support of the war effort either through rationing, volunteering, serving, or by buying war bonds. Although the Wichita factories produced planes for the Army, Wichitans also supported their country by staging war bond rallies. A 1944 rally featured this horse-drawn wagon. (Courtesy Wichita Public Library, Local History Section.)

After surviving the Depression years, the Beech Aircraft Company thrived during World War II with massive government contracts. Walter and Olive Ann Beech are shown looking over the production of AT-11 "Kansan" aircraft, derived from the commercial Model 18 and used for bomber training during the war. One of the AT-11's nicknames was "The Wichita Wobbler." (Courtesy Wichita Public Library, Local History Section.)

Aviation and agriculture were never far separated in Kansas. This AT-11 "Kansan" trainer is shown buzzing two combines during the summer wheat harvest. Aviation production, with its relatively high pay, drew tens of thousands to Wichita, which in turn caused a shortage of hands to work on Kansas's farms. (Courtesy Kansas Aviation Museum.)

The Beech Grizzly, inspired by the Model 18, was designed as a ground support with a 50-caliber machine gun mounted in the nose. The aircraft was fast and effective, but by the time it was ready for production, the war was ending and the days of the piston engine airplane were nearly over. Only the prototypes were ever produced. (Courtesy Kansas Aviation Museum.)

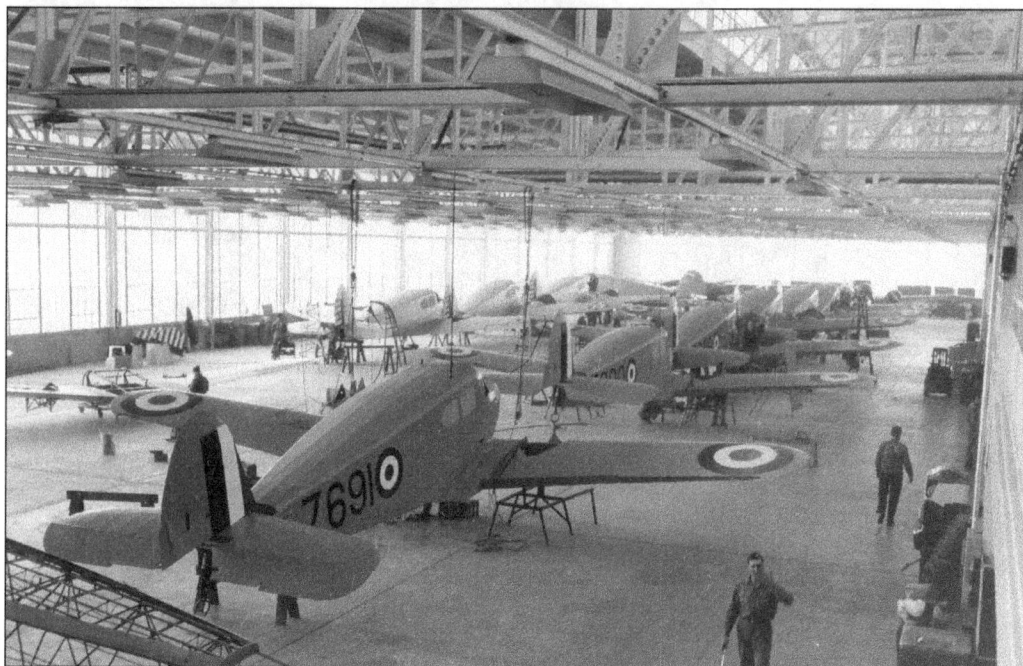

The Cessna production line swelled during World War II with military contracts. This aircraft, initially called the T-50 and later known as the UC-78, was one version of the Cessna Bobcat, produced for the military as a small transport plane. The plane was nicknamed the "Bamboo Bomber" because it was made of wood, steel, and fabric. Over 5,000 Bobcats were produced for the Army Air Force, the Navy, and, as shown here, the Royal Canadian Air Force (who called it the Crane 1). The plane was featured in the early television show *Sky King*. (Courtesy Kansas Aviation Museum.)

Of all the planes built in Wichita during World War II, the B-29 Superfortress had the greatest impact. Boeing Plant II was built for its production and nearly 30,000 employees, half of them women, participated in the manufacture of an estimated 1,400 of the bombers. When the war ended so did the production line. The unfinished aircraft were chopped up and hauled off and by 1946. Boeing employment dropped to 1,388 people. This picture depicts the company's celebration of the 1,000th B-29 produced. (Courtesy Kansas Aviation Museum.)

Wichita had its share of dedicated "Rosie the Riveters," as women replaced the men in the factories during the war years. They soon proved just as capable as the men of working around the clock producing the much-needed planes. (Courtesy Wichita Public Library, Local History Section.)

Cessna, in conjunction with Beech and Boeing, worked to produce 750 CG-4A transport gliders. for the Army Air Force This glider consisted of tubular steel, wood, and fabric and was capable of carrying 15 fully equipped fighting men. These gliders saw action in Burma, France, Holland, and Sicily. (Courtesy The Boeing Company.)

This picture shows Boeing Plant II, built for the production of B-29s, in the foreground, with the Planeview development nearest the plant and Hilltop Manor another mile farther north. Housing became a major problem in Wichita during World War II as the population boomed, mostly drawn by the tremendous demand for aircraft workers. The population boom brought many changes to Wichita: vocational training became available to quickly train aircraft workers, and women entered the workforce, replacing men who left for the war. In support of these workers, child-care became available for workers and schools operated year-round, offering crafts and activities after-hours to occupy children who had working parents. In addition, stores and businesses stayed open around the clock to support the 24-hour factory schedule. Entertainment venues such as the Orpheum had "'round the clock" scheduling of both stage and screen shows. Restaurants expanded their hours. Bowling alleys held early morning leagues for workers getting off the late shift. In addition, thousands of migrants, including African Americans and white southerners, came to Wichita, making the city more diverse. (Courtesy Kansas Aviation Museum.)

Three major government housing developments were constructed in Wichita during World War II. Although designed to be temporary, many of the buildings in two of the developments, Planeview and Hilltop Manor, are still standing and serve the community as low-cost housing. Beechwood, located near the Beech factory, was eventually razed. (Courtesy Wichita-Sedgwick County Historical Museum.)

After working long days in offices and manufacturing plants, a popular way to relax was going to the movies, especially when the theater was air-conditioned. The Miller Theater knew how to attract patrons, advertising "Refreshingly Cool" under its marquee. (Wichita-Sedgwick County Historical Museum.)

During the war years, Wichita became a 24-hour town, and one of its main thoroughfares, Douglas Avenue, always had some business open for the shift workers. (Courtesy Wichita Public Library, Local History Section.)

Patriotic displays such as this parade were common during World War II. This float displayed both Chinese and American flags and was sponsored by the Pan American Café, a local Chinese restaurant. Among the riders on the float was Wayne Wong, who served with the 14th Air Service Group in China. (Courtesy Wichita-Sedgwick County Historical Museum.)

The Pan American Café, located on North Market Street, opened its doors in the 1920s. The restaurant was founded by a partnership of Chinese immigrants and provided employment for many other Chinese immigrants, some of whom enlisted in the U.S. Army during World War II. The business also supported the war effort by staying open all night to serve late workers at the aircraft plants. (Courtesy Wichita-Sedgwick County Historical Museum.)

Entertainment for the public during the war years was extremely important for the morale of the nation. Wichitans could dance the evening away at the Shadowlands Dance Club located on North Hillside, in the former home of Swallow Aircraft Company. (Courtesy Wichita-Sedgwick County Historical Museum.)

Another popular spot in Wichita was the Blue Moon Club, where friends could gather around tables and socialize or dance or have their pictures taken by the roving photographer. Popular with aircraft workers, the Blue Moon also hosted well-known bands such as Glenn Miller's. (Courtesy Wichita-Sedgwick County Historical Museum.)

Patrons of the Blue Moon Club having a good time, discreetly keeping the liquor bottles under the table. (Courtesy Wichita-Sedgwick County Historical Museum.)

Three

COLD WAR BOOMTOWN

The 15 years following World War II transformed the entire country as production shifted from military to civilian needs and returning soldiers sought a place in the peacetime economy. This period was a particularly unsettled time in Wichita. The aviation industry had boomed during the war years but peacetime brought cutbacks and uncertainty. Some companies that thrived during the war, such as Culver, closed early in the postwar era. Many of the aircraft companies that remained introduced innovative small planes, hoping to find a new market in family transportation. While the dream of a plane in every garage never materialized, prosperity remained strong in Wichita thanks in part to companies' production of consumer goods and to the establishment of McConnell Air Force Base in 1954.

Wichita changed outside of the aircraft industry as well. Local companies such as Coleman kept the city economically diverse. New restaurants, hotels, institutions, and programs offered the population many leisure time activities. Change was political and social as well. No single event symbolizes Wichita's shifting structure better than the 1958 sit-in at Dockum's drug store that helped launch the civil rights movement in Wichita.

Throughout this time period, aviation retained its great influence. Employment returned to wartime peak levels by the mid-1950s, ensuring its prominent role in the coming years. As the 1950s ended, Wichita began a new decade by planning the first annual Mid-American Air Fair. Aviation continued to shape Wichita's future as it had the city's past.

The University Airport located at 25th and Hillside, shown here in 1946, was a scene for both social and aviation activity. (Courtesy Kansas Aviation Museum.)

In September 1945, fire gutted the Wichita Municipal Airport hangar. A fire engine and 27 airplanes were destroyed. The only air traffic controller on duty the day of the fire was Mary Chance VanScyoc. Mrs. VanScyoc was the first female aviation student at Wichita University and the first female air traffic controller in the United States. (Courtesy Wichita Public Library, Local History Section.)

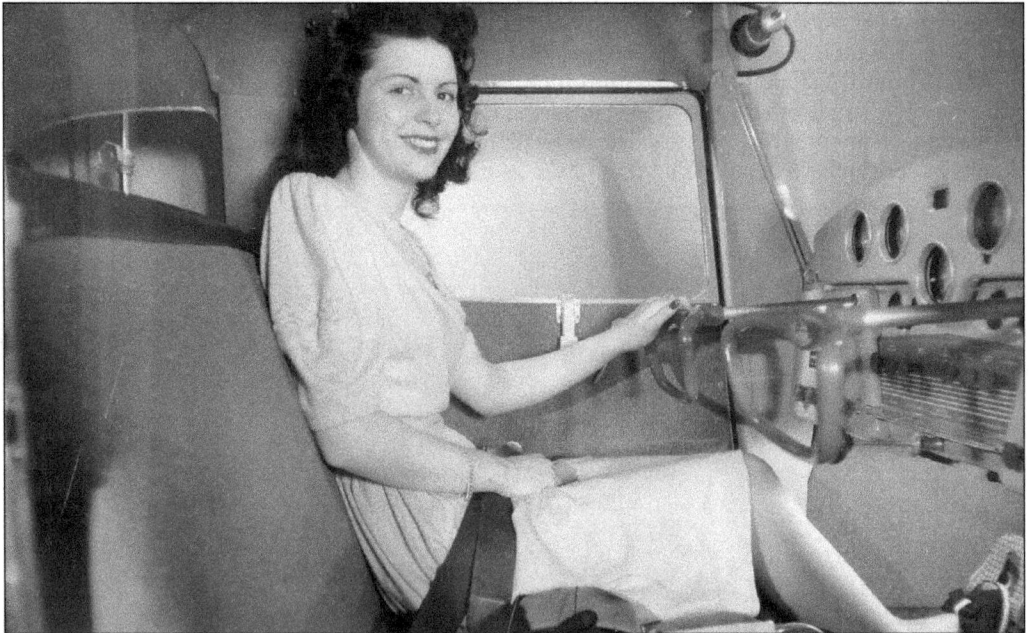

A female pilot sits in the cockpit of a Cessna 140 in this 1947 photo. The 140 was one of many models the aircraft industry introduced to capitalize on the postwar transition from military to civilian aviation production. By 1948, the expected market for consumer aircraft had not materialized, but the 140 and 140A remained popular into the 1950s. (Courtesy Kansas Aviation Museum.)

After the war, four Wichita aircraft companies—Beech, Boeing, Cessna, and Culver—began a foray into non-aircraft production. In 1946, Beech introduced a prototype automobile called the Plainsman. The vehicle had many new modern conveniences such as a telephone, four-wheel electric drive, and an aluminum body and frame. As its aircraft business improved, Beech abandoned the Plainsman, concluding it cost too much to produce. (Courtesy Kansas Aviation Museum.)

Actor Gregory Peck stopped in Wichita on July 16, 1946, showing a *Wichita Beacon* reporter a packet of promotional sunflower seeds for the film *Duel in the Sun*. The *Beacon* promoted the racy Western, nicknamed "Lust in the Dust," with a sunflower-growing contest. (Courtesy Kansas Aviation Museum.)

81 DRIVE-IN THEATRE

As the GIs returned home, many wanted to take their dates to the movies in an automobile. Drive-in theaters took off. The 81-Drive-in Theatre, located five miles north of Wichita on Broadway, billed itself as the city's first. Opened on August 15, 1946, under the ownership of O.F. Sullivan, the theater showed *Silver Skates*, *Belita*, and *Queen of the Ice* on its opening night. (Courtesy Wichita-Sedgwick County Historical Museum.)

In response to the housing shortage following the end of the war, designer R. Buckminster Fuller introduced his famous Dymaxion House concept. The idea was to ship pre-made aluminum parts in a small canister for rapid transport and assembly. Supposedly, aluminum was used because it could be mass-produced, easily shipped, and was hygienic and able to stand up to a Kansas tornado. If successful, aircraft companies, in this case, Beech, could have been in the house-building business. The name Dymaxion came from Waldo Warren, an advertising "wordsmith" who Marshall Field's & Company hired to come up with a name. Warren followed Fuller around for several days, noting Fuller's fondness for complex language. Stringing together such words as "dynamic," "maximum," and "tension" Warren created the word "Dymaxion." Fuller expected to construct 50,000 Dymaxion Houses, but Beech built only two prototypes. Of the two prototypes, one survives at the Henry Ford Museum & Greenfield Village in Michigan. (Courtesy Wichita-Sedgwick County Historical Museum.)

The glamour of aviation drew celebrities to Wichita for air shows, promotional tours, and aircraft purchases. Visitors learned to come to the airport to spot Hollywood stars passing through the city or having their planes serviced. Actor Robert Taylor (right), star of *Camille* and *Ivanhoe*, appears here with his Beech. Taylor's connection to aviation began during World War II, when he served in the Navy as a flight instructor for the Air Transport Division. (Courtesy Kansas Aviation Museum.)

Standing in front of a Boeing L-15 Scout Aircraft, General Dwight D. Eisenhower congratulated two Native American Boeing employees, Gordon Bushyhead and Francis Stumbling Bear, at the Boeing-Wichita Plant in January 1948. At right is J. Earl Schaefer, Boeing general manager from 1932–1957, who was also a cadet with General Eisenhower at West Point. (Courtesy Wichita Public Library, Local History Section.)

Postwar leisure activities gave civilians a chance to see the items their military counterparts had encountered. In this 1948 photo a crowd of curious onlookers gathers at the Forum to view a German 88 mm anti-aircraft cannon called "Tiny." (Courtesy Wichita Public Library, Local History Section.)

The relationship between Wichita and Orleans, France, extended back to World War II, when the 137th Infantry Division liberated the city. Many of the troops in the 137th were from Wichita. The official relationship between the two cities began in 1949 with a week-long swap of Mayor William Salome, Jr. and Deputy Mayor Jean Falaize. As a sign of friendship, the children of Wichita paid for the construction of a miniature train for Orleans. The Chance Company of Wichita built the train, and to finance it children paid 10 cents to ride on it once it was completed. The gift went to France in 1951 with the word "friendship" on the train in both English and French. A duplicate version operated at Wichita's "Joyland" amusement park for years. (Courtesy Wichita Public Library, Local History Section.)

With its aircraft industry growing again and the economy getting stronger, the city of Wichita began to grow physically. New housing communities started to appear, traffic jams became worse, and the city's infrastructure was stressed to its limits. Underneath all of this postwar expansion and prosperity, though, the Cold War was heating up and Wichita played a huge role in it. (Courtesy Wichita Public Library, Local History Section.)

Coleman's first focus was rural lighting and heating, but by the 1950s the company had diversified into space heaters and air conditioners. By the 1960s, production facilities included West Germany and the Netherlands as well as Wichita. (Courtesy Wichita Public Library, Local History Section.)

Air Force personnel stand in front of a Boeing B-47 Stratojet bomber. In June of 1951, the Air Force established a base in Wichita located on the east side of the municipal airport to train B-47 pilots. Initially called the Wichita Air Force Base, it eventually became McConnell Air Force Base. From 1951 to 1958 the Air Training Command's 3520th Combat Crew Training Wing trained Boeing B-47 Stratojet bomber air crews. (Courtesy Kansas Aviation Museum.)

From Coleman's original headquarters at First and St. Francis, the company produced such products as their world-famous portable stoves and lanterns. In 1962, it produced its 15 millionth lantern. From its early days, Coleman capitalized on the aviation industry for shipping its products around the country. (Courtesy Wichita Public Library, Local History Section.)

The transformation of America's economy in the years after World War II affected Wichita's job market and the look of the city as well. The construction of the Woolworth Building in downtown Wichita started in 1948. (Courtesy Wichita Public Library, Local History Section.)

The Red Apple
Restaurant and
Grocery, operated
by the Reynolds
family, was located on
3421 North Broadway.
To the left of the
business was a Conoco
filling station and
to the right, a root
beer stand. The green
stem of the apple was
actually a smokestack.
This photo shows
the Red Apple after
it closed in 1950.
(Courtesy Wichita
Public Library, Local
History Section.)

Built in 1949 at Oliver and Douglas, Lincoln Heights Village was one of the first shopping centers in Wichita. Shown here in a modern photograph, Lincoln Heights catered to shoppers who drove in from growing suburban neighborhoods such as Crown Heights or the nearby community of Eastborough. (Courtesy Jay M. Price.)

This is an aerial view of the University of Wichita in 1949. As with most colleges in the United States, the postwar years changed the campus. This change included returning servicemen taking advantage of the educational provisions of the GI Bill and education's shift in emphasis to the sciences. The remodeled version of the stadium at the top is today known as "Cessna Stadium." (Courtesy Wichita Public Library, Local History Section.)

Wichitan James Jabara joined the Army Air Corps in 1943. He flew P-51 Mustangs while stationed in Europe. During the Korean War, Jabara became the first jet ace fighter pilot in history. Upon Jabara's return to the United States, Wichita welcomed him with a parade in his honor. He shot down nine more MIGs after returning to Korea. (Courtesy Wichita-Sedgwick County Historical Museum.)

The city sponsored fishing derbies for all ages; the crowded shore of this 1957 derby at Airport Lakes indicates the popularity of such events with citizens. (Courtesy Wichita Public Library, Local History Section.)

School organizations in elementary schools included traffic patrols in Wichita. Here, a group of young boys pose with their equipment in front of their school. (Courtesy Wichita Public Library, Local History Section.)

In 1953, entrepreneur J.C. Squier had a grass airstrip put in at Beaumont, Kansas, so that pilots of small aircraft flying east to the Flint Hills community could eat and stay at the local hotel. Beaumont was a short flight from Wichita and allowed pilots to taxi along one of the main streets and park their planes in front of the hotel, as in this recent photo. (Courtesy Jay M. Price.)

Like many students in the United States during the Cold War, students in Wichita prepared for a nuclear attack. The aircraft industry in the area increased the possibility that Wichita would be a target. (Courtesy Wichita Public Library, Local History Section.)

Another Civil Defense institution was the "block mother," whose home was open to neighborhood children during an emergency or attack. A sign notified children of this house in which they could take shelter. (Courtesy Wichita Public Library, Local History Section.)

Douglas Avenue appears here in the winter of 1951. In 1958, the Dockum Drug store in the background became the site of one of the first successful student sit-ins in American history. Members of the Wichita NAACP Youth Council organized the peaceful protest two years before the much-publicized sit-in in Greensboro, North Carolina. Dockum's parent drugstore chain, Rexall, began integrated service as a result of the Wichita sit-in's effect on business. (Courtesy Wichita Public Library, Local History Section.)

Many towns in the United States included a library system with a bookmobile. The segregation that existed in the Wichita school system can clearly be seen in these two photographs. The 1954 Supreme Court case of *Brown v. Board of Education of Topeka, Kansas,* marked the end of legal school segregation nationwide, including in Wichita. By 1960, though, fewer than half of Wichita's schools were integrated. (Courtesy Wichita Public Library, Local History Section.)

Here a "story lady" entertains a group of African American students in McKinley Park in 1952. (Courtesy Wichita Public Library, Local History Section.)

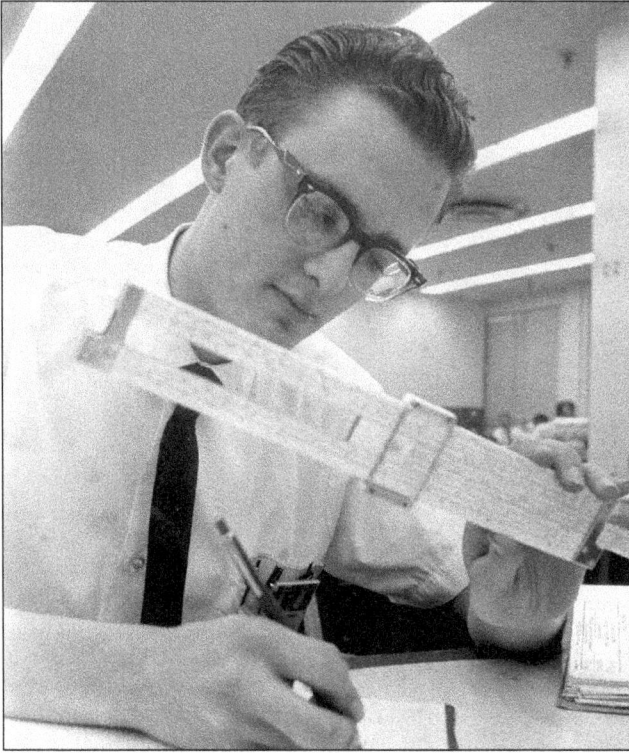

Here a Boeing engineer uses a slide rule for calculations. With advancements in aviation, the scientific knowledge required to build aircraft increased. This trend in aircraft production accelerated with the heightening of the Cold War during the 1950s and 1960s. (Courtesy Wichita Public Library, Local History Section.)

Over the skies of Wichita, Boeing B-29s conduct aerial refueling tests on March 28, 1948. (Courtesy Wichita-Sedgwick County Historical Museum.)

Visitors relax in the lobby of the Hamilton Hotel, located on South Main, in this 1958 photo. The calendar on the wall was a reminder of aviation's influence on the city. (Courtesy Wichita Public Library, Local History Section.)

Charles M. Seibel, a pioneer in helicopter design, introduced the first of his innovative aircraft in 1950. The Seibel S-4A (above, with Seibel at the controls) was much less expensive and easier to fly than other helicopters. Its success reflected the increasing popularity of small personal aircraft. When Cessna bought Seibel's company two years later, he led its helicopter division. (Courtesy Wichita Public Library, Local History Section.)

Kansas Republican women met in Washington D.C. with then-Vice President Richard M. Nixon and wife Pat (center) in 1958. Kansans identified with both Nixon and President Dwight D. Eisenhower because of Eisenhower's roots in Abilene. (Courtesy Wichita State University Libraries, Department of Special Collections.)

92

The Beech Bonanza, first sold in 1947, was intended to fill the demands of the expected postwar market for personal aircraft. Although this market did not develop as anticipated, the Bonanza remained in production until 1982, making it among the longest continuously produced airplane models. Its comfort and durability ensured its popularity, and the unusual V-shaped tail made the Bonanza easily identifiable. (Courtesy Kansas Aviation Museum.)

The Air Force established a base in Wichita and, on May 15, 1954, dedicated it to the McConnell brothers, locals who had served in the Army Air Forces during World War II. McConnell Air Force Base was initially intended to honor only Thomas (left) and Fred (right), who had been killed in plane crashes. In 1999, two years after his death, Edwin (center) was finally included with the base's rededication. (Courtesy Kansas Aviation Museum.)

With the Air Force's decision to create a base in Wichita came an urgent need to house the men coming to serve. The wartime housing district of Planeview, just north of the city airport, was offered as a location. In June 1951, after only a month of construction, 2,000 men lived in canvas tents on wooden platforms (above). Nearby, Wichita's three wartime housing communities of Beechwood, Planeview, and Hilltop Manor housed workers and became close-knit communities. McConnell Air Force Base affected the face of Wichita as well, with its annual payroll of $18 million and movement of thousands into the area. By 1956, McConnell saw more air traffic than any other military airport in the country. Two years later, the complex grew larger when it became a Strategic Air Command base. (Courtesy Kansas Aviation Museum.)

Boeing, like other aircraft manufacturers, suffered economically immediately after the end of World War II, but military contracts revitalized the company. Plant II closed after the war, but in 1948 it reopened for construction of the innovative B-47 bomber, the first jet produced in the city of Wichita. Before production ended in 1956, more than two-thirds of the B-47s built came out of the Wichita facility. B-47 pilots trained right across the street from Boeing Wichita's manufacturing plant. The beginning of the Korean War created demand for Kansas' aircraft. In 1951, Boeing subcontracted $90 million throughout Kansas. Three years later, the company employed 30,000 workers, equal to its wartime peak. The manufacturing facility shown above employed a greater number of people than all but six cities in Kansas. Boeing became the United States' largest defense contractor in 1957. (Courtesy Kansas Aviation Museum.)

The Boeing Bombers, Boeing Wichita's associated baseball team, won the National Baseball Congress championship in 1942, 1954, and 1955. The league for nonprofessional adult players, organized by Wichitan Hap Dumont in 1931, held its first major tournament in 1935. The Boeing Bombers were typical of teams that played in the NBC's early decades: they were sponsored by a company and many players on the roster were former professionals, and all were employees of the company. (Courtesy Wichita State University Libraries, Department of Special Collections.)

The city's nightlife united with the aviation industry in this 1957 Cessna Air Show that featured musicians along with the newest aircraft. Aviation had an influence on Wichita after hours, just as it did during the workday. (Courtesy Wichita State University Libraries, Department of Special Collections.)

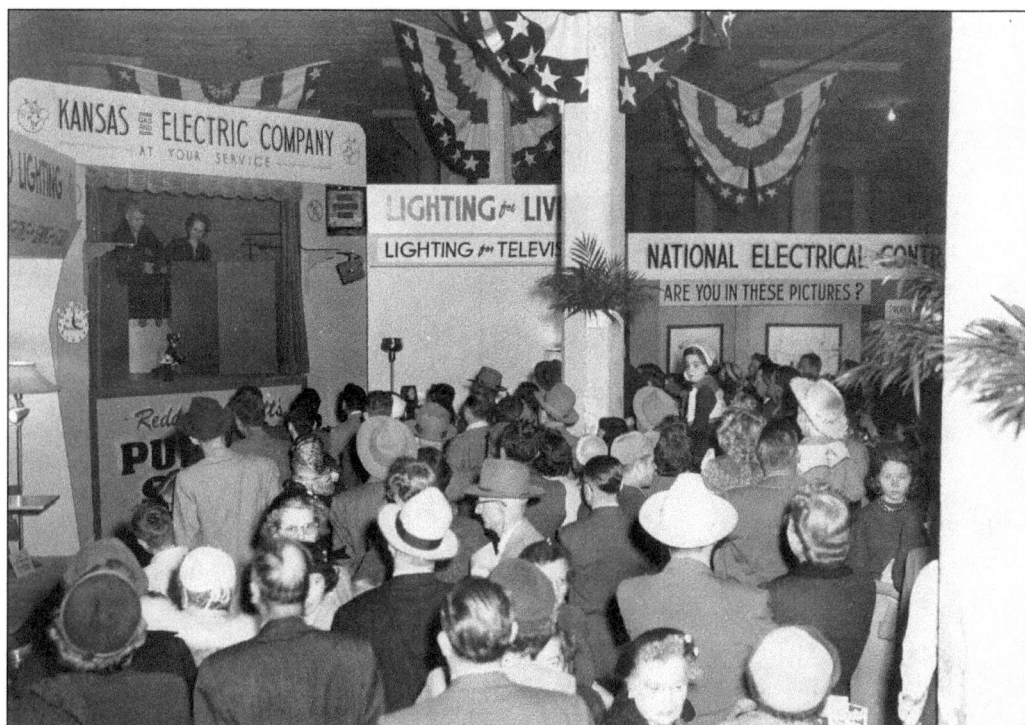

The 1955 Greater Wichita Home Show showcased the city's innovations outside aviation, drawing a crowd to exhibits introducing the cutting edge of local and national industry. A similar event still takes place annually. (Courtesy Wichita Public Library, Local History Section.)

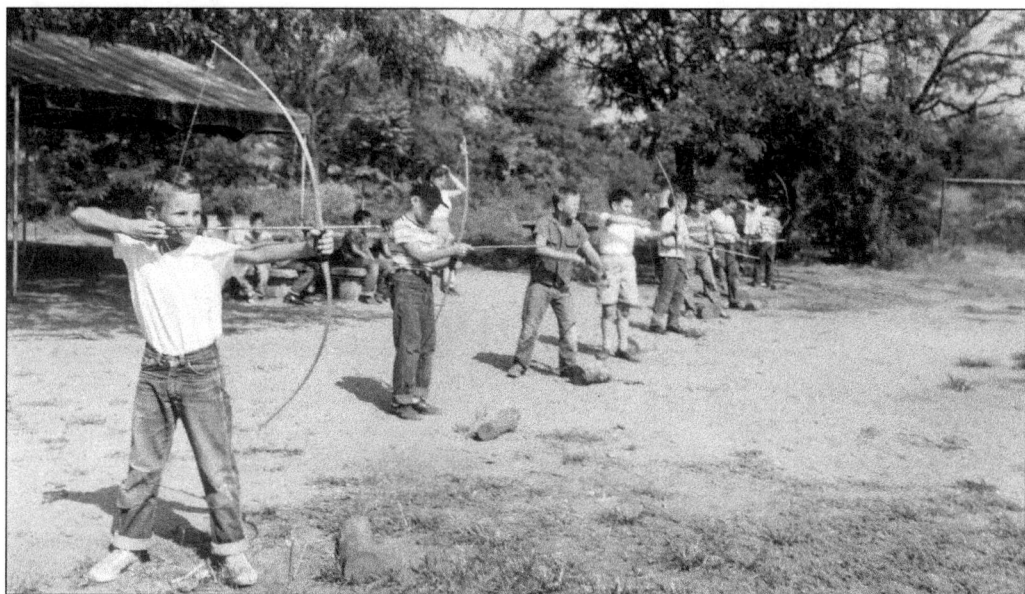

Wichita sponsored a number of social and cultural activities in the 1950s, motivated to serve the increasing population. Such recreational programs were for all age groups. The Wichita Parks Department took this photo of a boys' day camp in July 1957. (Courtesy Wichita Public Library, Local History Section.)

Wichita produced the Boeing B-52D Stratofortress from 1956 to 1962. Of 744 B-52s built, 467 were assembled in Wichita and the remainder in Seattle. The bomber could transport 60,000 pounds of weapons, including four hydrogen bombs, and was used in the Vietnam conflict and in the Persian Gulf. (Courtesy Wichita Public Library, Local History Section.)

With the beginning of a new decade, Wichitans looked forward to a continuation of aviation's important role. Above, A.K. "Al" Wilson (left) and E. Charles Straub meet on March 31, 1960, to work on plans for the first annual Mid-American Air Fair, to be held at the Wichita Municipal Airport from April 8 to 10. Wilson was the chair of the Chamber of Commerce's aviation committee, and Straub had been the airport's manager since 1941. He had seen it through a devastating fire and a move to new facilities in 1954 after the Air Force grew into and purchased Wichita's former airport. As the 1960s began, change and adaptation continued to shape the development of the city's definitive industry—in its facilities, its publicity, and its innovation. (Courtesy Wichita Public Library, Local History Section.)

The City of Wichita built its new airport terminal in 1960. Wichita Municipal Airport moved to the southwest side of the city after McConnell Air Force Base took over the former facility in 1954. The airport became Wichita Mid-Continent Airport in 1973 and underwent another major remodeling program in the mid-1980s. By 1985, the facility was served by eight major airlines, although tough economic times saw the demise of some mainstays in commercial aviation. (Courtesy Wichita-Sedgwick County Historical Museum.)

Four

SOARING INTO THE
NEXT CENTURY

The jet age had arrived. The military had been using jet fighters since the 1950s and commercial jet liners such as Boeing's 707 had become the standard by 1960. The jumbo jet was on the horizon as was the world's smallest jet, built by Newton, Kansas resident James Bede. Aviation's detractors constantly voiced concern that Wichita was too dependent on the industry, but Wichita continued to be the Air Capital.

The Cold War and the threat of nuclear conflict still held the planet in its grip. The conflicts in Southeast Asia heated up and tensions escalated in the Middle East as well as other parts of the world—not to mention the racial and social tensions that tore at the fabric of American society. Changing economic patterns dramatically altered employment in the aviation industry in Wichita. Mergers and takeovers forever changed the landscape of aviation.

American companies in the 1980s struggled to compete in a world market that they had heretofore dominated. Airline deregulation and economic chaos in the 1970s bankrupted companies like Braniff, Eastern, and Frontier, while local companies like Ryan Aviation (later Ryan International) and Yingling Aircraft thrived. Wichita prospered from the companies that survived and saw more people than ever take to the skies in the 1990s.

The attacks on the Pentagon and World Trade Center on September 11, 2001 devastated the aviation community economically as well as emotionally. In light of these events and other changes in international aviation, Wichita dealt with crippling layoffs while the companies reassessed their goals and their products. Once again, the city asked itself if it had become too dependent upon one industry. Others insisted that this was simply the latest instance of Wichita reinventing itself. As the 21st century dawned, Wichita found itself in a situation not unlike that of a century ago: a community whose entrepreneurial spirit yearned to harness the changes sweeping in like the Kansas wind.

Pictured above is the Learjet 40. (Courtesy Bombardier Aerospace.)

Bill Lear rocked the aviation world in 1962 when he announced his Swiss-based company's move to Wichita. He thought that Wichita offered the best people to design and build his personal business jet, saying European designers "lacked originality and imagination." He sold the company to Gates Rubber Company in 1967. (Courtesy Wichita Public Library, Local History Section.)

The idea of a small business jet had been around since the 1950s, but Learjet set the standard when its first plane was certified for flight in 1964. Lear's clientele literally spanned the globe and included foreign dignitaries such as Jordan's King Hussein. These aircraft were so well associated with their type that small business jets were often referred to as "Learjets" regardless of their make. (Courtesy Wichita Public Library, Local History Section.)

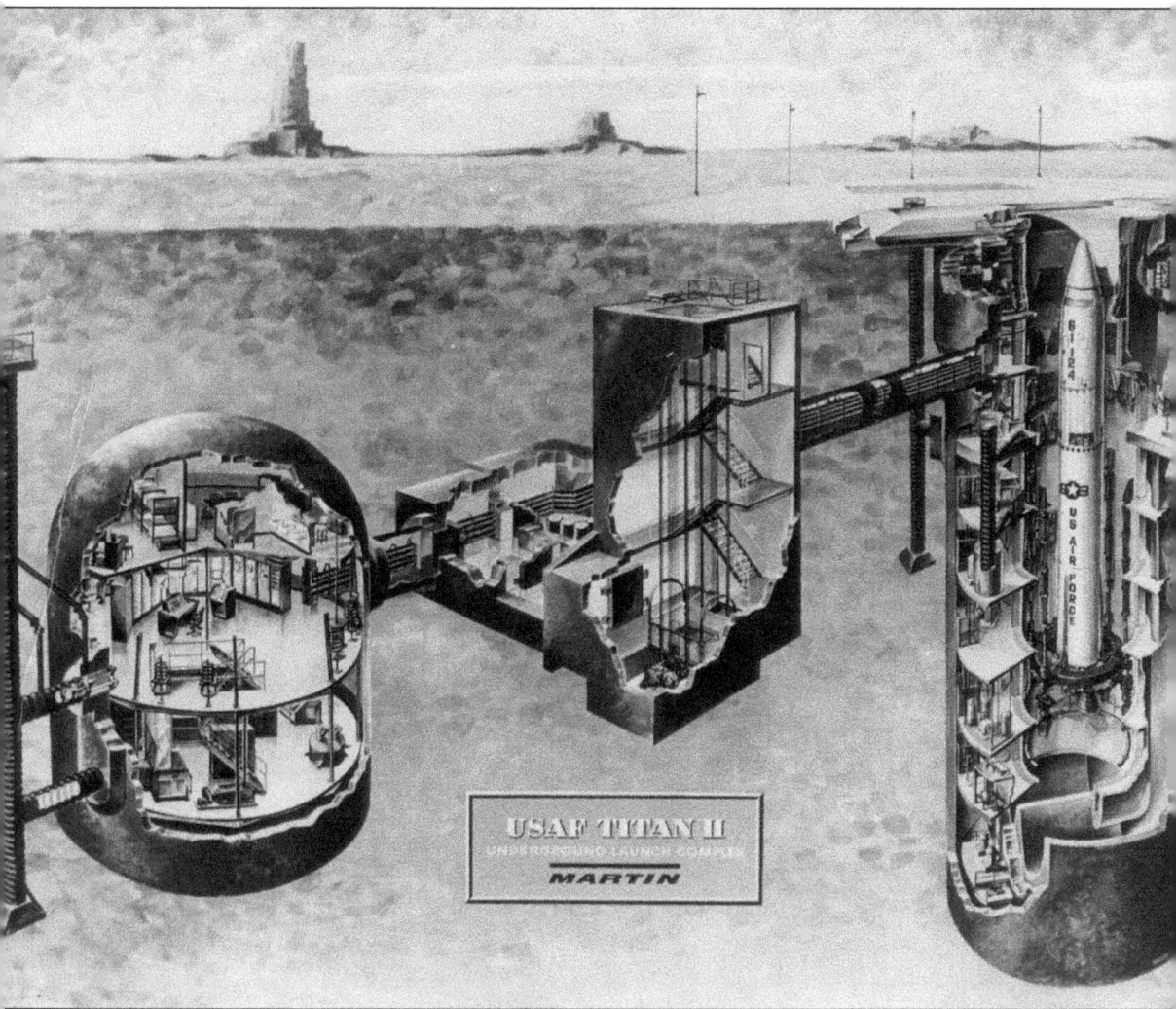

This drawing shows the 160 foot missile silo as well as the crew and support areas of a Titan II missile complex. The first of 18 Titan II Intercontinental Ballistic Missile sites was constructed near Wichita in 1960. The 381st Strategic Missile Wing at McConnell Air Force Base was activated on March 1, 1962. (Courtesy Kansas Aviation Museum.)

Newer strategic missile systems made the Titan II obsolete by 1981 and the 381st Strategic Missile Wing was deactivated August 8, 1986. This nose cone was from one of the inactivated Titan IIs surrounding Wichita. It is now on permanent display at McConnell Air Force Base. (Courtesy John D. Hays.)

Families of military personnel must deal with frequent and sometimes long separations. Family members welcome home their loved ones from a tour of duty. (Courtesy Wichita-Sedgwick County Historical Museum.)

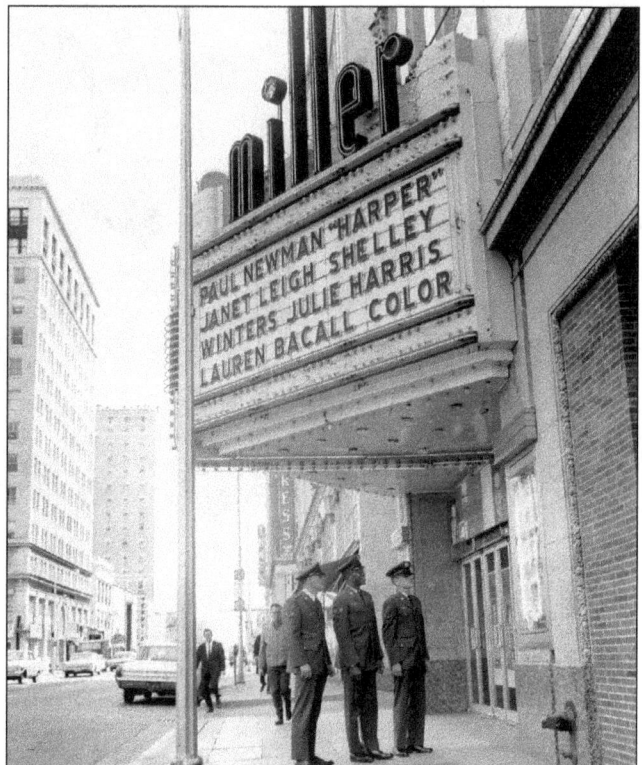

Three airmen from McConnell Air Force Base prepare to see a movie at the Miller Theater at 121 North Broadway in 1966. The photo illustrates not only the importance of the base to the community but also ethnic diversity in times of racial tension. (Courtesy Wichita State University Libraries, Department of Special Collections.)

The Air Capital Memorial Park welcomed visitors to west Wichita on U.S. 54 highway from 1969 to 1988. This B-47E was the centerpiece of the park, where it sat on V-shaped pylons. It was moved to McConnell AFB in 1988, after an extensive restoration to remove over 53 bullet holes due to vandalism. It was moved a second time to McConnell's main gate in 1999 after another restoration. (Courtesy John D. Hays.)

Lieutenant Ted Coukoulis meets Brigadier General Edward R. Fry as McConnell Air Force Base takes delivery of its first F-105 Thunderchief. A few years earlier, the 388th Fighter Wing was stationed at McConnell Air Force Base. The wing trained in Wichita and later saw much action in Vietnam. (Courtesy Wichita State University Libraries, Department of Special Collections.)

A natural gas explosion disrupted a 1964 labor strike at Boeing. The explosion damaged several parked cars and injured one demonstrator. (Courtesy Wichita State University Libraries, Department of Special Collections.)

Vietnam-era demonstrations took place in Wichita as elsewhere in the United States. Demonstrators march down 17th Street just south of the Wichita State University main campus. (Courtesy Wichita State University Libraries, Department of Special Collections.)

Tragedy struck a northwest Wichita community on January 16, 1965, when a fully-loaded KC-135A tanker took off from McConnell AFB at 9:28 a.m. and crashed at 20th and Piatt three minutes later. Thirty people, including the six crew members, twenty-three residents, and one unborn baby, died from the crash that destroyed 16 homes. (Courtesy *Wichita Eagle and Beacon* Publishing Company.)

The City of Wichita established Piatt Park on the site of the KC-135A crash in 1971. 20th and Piatt was, and remains, predominantly an African-American neighborhood near Wichita State University. (Courtesy John D. Hays.)

The 384th Air Refueling Wing arrived at McConnell in June of 1971. It was the first unit to receive the KC-135R Stratotanker throughout its entire fleet on August 5, 1987. The KC-135R was fitted with quieter, more efficient engines. Pictured above is a KC-135A tanker refueling a B-52 bomber. (Courtesy Kansas Aviation Museum.)

This is an interior view of the refueling procedure aboard a KC-135A. The boom operator is in radio contact with the pilot of the aircraft being fueled, and is charge of both aircraft during fueling. The boom swings down from the aft fuselage of the tanker and fits into a special receiver valve on the other aircraft. This responsibility gives boom operators, who can hold any rank from airman to master sergeant, an unusual amount of authority for an enlisted person. (Courtesy Kansas Aviation Museum.)

Ingalls Elementary School student Carl Tucker presents a sympathy card signed by fellow students to Wichita State University President Clark Ahlberg along with their contributions to the Football '70 Memorial Fund. On October 2, 1970, an airplane carrying the Wichita State University football team crashed in Colorado Rocky Mountains killing 31 team members, supporters, coaches, and airline personnel. (Courtesy Wichita State University Libraries, Department of Special Collections.)

Refugees from Southeast Asia began immigrating to Wichita in 1975 following the Vietnam conflict. Many of them settled in the Planeview area in south Wichita. Pictured is the Southeast Asian Baptist Church, located on South Hillside. Its congregation is predominately Laotian. (Courtesy John D. Hays.)

The Cessna Sky Hawk began production in 1956 and became the most popular light plane ever built. Here workers assemble the planes in the company's Pawnee Plant in the 1970s. (Courtesy Wichita Public Library, Local History Section.)

1975 CESSNA SKYHAWK -- 100,000TH SINGLE-ENGINE AIRPLANE PRODUCED BY CESSNA PAWNEE DIVISION

Cessna produced this Sky Hawk in 1975. It was the 100,000th single-engine aircraft produced at the Pawnee plant. (Courtesy Wichita Public Library, Local History Section.)

Dwane Wallace was instrumental in reopening the Cessna Aircraft Company in 1934. He was one of the first to see the need for a small business jet in the 1960s that was more affordable than the Learjet and Lockheed Jetstar. The answer became the Cessna Citation jet. (Courtesy Cessna Aircraft Company.)

> Last night I lay me down to sleep,
> But dreams of Cessna began to creep
> Into my poor befuddled mind,
> And what do I awake to find?
>
> My Cessna, she is here no more.
> What once was now is gone before.
> No jigs, no tools, no merry men,
> Alas, alack, just Olive Ann.
>
> (Dwane Wallace Scrapbook, Kansas Aviation Museum.)

Rumors of takeovers between Cessna and Beech abounded in the 1970s and 1980s, as each company vied for its place in the world of aviation. This poem appeared in an internal publication for Cessna. (Courtesy Kansas Aviation Museum.)

The City of Wichita wanted to expand its convention business in the 1960s. The answer was Century II, which housed halls for conventions, concerts, and the theater. Construction began in 1966 and was completed in 1971. A 1984 addition nearly tripled the amount of available convention space. To make room for the structure, 116 buildings were removed. One was the Wichita Forum, which had served as a showplace for theater, opera, and the occasional livestock show for 50 years. Century II houses the Wichita Symphony, Wichita Pops Orchestra, Music Theater of Wichita, and the New York Paramount Wurlitzer pipe organ. (Courtesy Wichita Public Library, Local History Section.)

Air shows and airplane displays have been a part of Wichita since the early days of aviation. This photo shows a crowd gathered to admire *Fifi*, a fully restored B-29 bomber. The Texas-based Confederate Air Force restored her to flying condition. The exhibit took place at Mid-Continent Airport in the 1980s. (Courtesy John D. Hays.)

Air Force F-4 Phantom jets fly over a crowd at a McConnell Air Force Base air show in the 1970s. The show was one of several in Wichita over the years to feature the Air Force Thunderbirds aerial demonstration team. (Courtesy Wichita-Sedgwick County Historical Museum.)

114

Wichitans celebrate a block party in Wichita's Old Town during the 1999 River Festival. The celebration was started in 1972 to celebrate the Arkansas (ar-KAN-sas) River. (Courtesy Harry Adams through Wichita State University Libraries, Department of Special Collections.)

The 1980s and 1990s were a turbulent time for Wichita aircraft companies. General Dynamics bought Cessna Aircraft Company in 1985 and then sold it to Textron in 1992. Pictured above is one of the newest aircraft from Cessna, the Citation Excel. (Courtesy Cessna Aircraft Company.)

OH HAPPY DAY!

Olive Ann Beech's employees used "mood flags," such as the one above, to gauge her daily emotions. Flags ranged from "happy" to "lightning" to "surprise." (Courtesy Wichita State University Libraries, Department of Special Collections.)

Olive Ann Beech was one of the most respected women in aviation. She was a model for future generations of female business executives, chairing Beech from Walter's death in 1950 until her retirement in 1983. In addition to running the company, Olive Ann hosted celebrities visiting Wichita, such as Bob Hope. (Courtesy Raytheon Aviation.)

The Beech Starship paved the way for the use of composite materials for strong and lightweight construction. It was designed to compete with small business jets, but the cost was often higher. It entered service in 1992, but was discontinued in 1994. There were only 53 produced. (Courtesy Kansas Aviation Museum.)

Bombardier vice-president of flight test Pete Reynolds (left), flight test engineer Eric Nordberg (center), and engineering test pilot Doug May (right) set a record on their flight from Wichita to Orlando, Florida, on September 10, 2002, in their Learjet 40. The flight took 2 hours and 39 minutes with just over 10 hours of flight time on the aircraft. Gates Learjet became part of Bombardier Aerospace in 1990. (Courtesy Bombardier Aerospace.)

High airfares at Mid-Continent Airport prompted many travelers to drive to Kansas City or Oklahoma City, where the fares were cheaper. The airlines cited high airport fees and low numbers of travelers as reasons for the higher fares. The city of Wichita countered this trend by enticing discount air carriers to Wichita. One such carrier was Vanguard Airlines, which operated in Wichita for two years, beginning in April of 1995. Recently, Air Tran Airlines and Frontier Airlines arrived as discount carriers. (Courtesy Wichita Public Library, Local History Section.)

Savute's, an Italian restaurant at 3303 North Broadway, has served the Wichita community since the 1950s. The mural on the north side of the building depicts the importance of aviation to the city. The Stick and Rudder Club inside the restaurant building contains photographs and other aircraft memorabilia. (Courtesy Delsa Hays.)

Frank and Dan Carney, two University of Wichita students, founded Pizza Hut in 1958 and watched it grow into the largest pizza chain in the world. The familiar red roof on this restaurant became the standard in 1969. (Courtesy John D. Hays.)

The Boeing 747 made its debut flight on February 9, 1969, ushering in the era of the jumbo jet. The first 747 entered service with Pan American Airlines in 1970. This VC-25A, commonly known as Air Force One, is a modified 747-200B that entered service in 1990. The two aircraft that comprise the presidential fleet were assembled in Seattle and modified in Wichita. Boeing Wichita provided the nosepieces for the 747. Two other local companies, Hiller and Precision Patterns Inc., were responsible for much of the interior work on Air Force One.(Courtesy The Boeing Company.)

Pictured above are golfers at the 2001 Bomhoff Open held at Pawnee Prairie Golf Course (recently renamed for "Mr. Golf in Wichita," Tex Consolver.) Bomhoff, a manufacturer of custom aircraft interiors, was sold to Tulsa-based Nordam in 2002. (Courtesy Russ De Vasure.)

The 384th Bombardment Wing (Heavy) was activated on July 1, 1987, and became one of four units assigned the B-1B bomber in 1988. The B-1 Market, located just north of McConnell on Rock Road, was one of the many businesses in Wichita that reflected the importance of aviation to the community. The bomber wing brought an influx of jobs and revenue to the city. The B-1Bs were transferred to the Kansas Air National Guard in 1994, the first Air National Guard unit ever to be assigned heavy bombers. (Courtesy John D. Hays.)

The "Bee 1 Bomber," built for the "the Sculptors of the Plains" project, was one of 31 whimsical airplane sculptures in the "Plane Crazy" art project. Wichita's Arts Council sponsored the project to commemorate the 100th anniversary of flight in 2003. The real B-1Bs left Wichita in 2002, when the 184th Bomb Wing became the 184th Refueling Wing. Just days before its transfer, the wing tied a record for sorties in order to demonstrate its capabilities and willingness to stay in Wichita. (Courtesy John D. Hays.)

Wichita native Dan Glickman was instrumental in the passage of the General Aviation Revitalization Act of 1994. This act limited the liability of manufacturers of small aircraft and breathed new life into that floundering segment of the industry. Glickman served in the U.S. House of Representatives from 1977 to 1995 and as Secretary of Agriculture from 1995 until 2002. (Courtesy United States Department of Agriculture.)

The General Aviation Revitalization Act reduced liability claims on small aircraft. The manufacture of planes such as this Cessna Stationair resumed. (Courtesy Wichita Public Library, Local History Section.)

Bob Knight finished his seventh term as Mayor of Wichita in 2002. He campaigned for his first city council seat in 1979 with a platform of fair taxation and anti-racist policies. Knight was an avid supporter of globalizing Wichita and lobbied heavily to entice travelers to use Mid-Continent Airport. He was instrumental in the city's decision to subsidize Air Tran Airlines and Frontier Airlines. (Courtesy City of Wichita.)

Senator Bob Dole of Kansas celebrates the opening of Air Tran at Mid-Continent on May 8, 2002, with an Air Tran at Mid Continent Airport crew. The Orlando, Florida-based airline was guaranteed subsidies from the City of Wichita for two years in return for reduced airfares from Wichita so that travelers would "Ditch the Drive" to Kansas City and Oklahoma City airports. (Courtesy Air Tran.)

The former Wichita Municipal Airport building became the home of the Kansas Aviation Museum in 1990. The building had fallen into disrepair, but volunteers repaired the building, maintained the archives of many of Wichita's aviation facilities, and housed and restored aircraft designed or built in Kansas. (Courtesy John D. Hays.)

Doc, a B-29 bomber, was rescued from the junk pile and began a process of complete restoration in May of 2000. Boeing Wichita provided the hangar space to house the restoration. Area aerospace workers, retirees, and others volunteered their time to complete it. Many manufacturers donated parts and materials free or at a reduced rate. When finished, it will be one of two B-29s in flying condition and the only B-29 to undergo a complete rebuild. (Courtesy The Boeing Company.)

Wichita has prided itself on aviation research since the earliest days of flight. The National Institute of Aviation Research was built on the campus of Wichita State University in 1985. The Federal Aviation Administration selected NIAR to be one of nine core members of the Airworthiness Assurance Center of Excellence in September 1997, and received the FAA Excellence in Aviation institutional award in 2001. (Courtesy John D. Hays.)

WSU students Monal P. Merchant (left) and Tejas N. Mazmudar stand beside the "3x4" wind tunnel in the NIAR building. Their project studied thermal effects on composite materials in general aviation aircraft and was funded through NASA and the FAA. WSU students constructed the "3x4" wind tunnel in 1985. It is a low-speed wind tunnel used for the study of sub-sonic conditions of objects from aircraft to trash cans. (Courtesy John D. Hays.)

Corporations from Spain, France, Germany, and Great Britain formed Airbus in 1970 through a cooperative effort. It had achieved its goal of competing with U.S. aircraft companies by the 1990s but was criticized by some American companies because of its subsidies from European governments. Airbus took advantage of the slow economic climate and available engineering expertise in Wichita to build its engineering facility there in June of 2002. (Courtesy John D. Hays.)

This cartoon comments on the differing opinions Wichita workers had regarding Airbus's entrance to the area. (Courtesy Richard Crowson and *Wichita Eagle and Beacon* Publishing Company.)

126

U.S. President Bill Clinton visited workers at Cessna's 21st Street Project in November 1997. His was the sixth visit of a sitting president to Wichita. In the center is Cessna head Russ Meyer. The "welfare to work" program opened in 1990 to offset the economic gap between Wichitans with jobs and those considered unemployable. The program was designed to reduce residents' dependence on government support. The new 21st Street campus building was built in 1997 to expand the program. (Courtesy Wichita State University Libraries, Department of Special Collections.)

Aviation even impacted religion in Wichita. Temple Emanu-El had this jet-shaped menorah available for those who wanted a suitably "Wichitan" Hanukkah celebration. (Courtesy Jay M. Price.)

Lawrence Dumont Stadium (foreground) is the second-oldest baseball stadium in the Texas League. It hosted the Aeroes from 1970 to 1984, and the Wichita Pilots from 1987 to 1988. The team became the Wichita Wranglers in 1989. This photograph also shows the Arkansas River, the Hyatt-Regency Hotel, and Century II. As the city looks forward to its second century of aviation, it builds on a rich tradition of ingenuity, hard work, and adaptation to change. (Courtesy Les Broadstreet through Wichita State University Libraries, Department of Special Collections.)

Visit us at
arcadiapublishing.com

·····························